MONSTER FIGHT CLUB
SUPERNATURAL CREATURES

ANITA GANERI AND DAVID WEST

PowerKiDS
press
New York

Published in 2012 by The Rosen Publishing Group, Inc.
29 East 21st Street, New York, NY 10010

Designed and produced by
David West Books

Designer and illustrator: David West
Editor: Ronne Randall

Library of Congress Cataloging-in-Publication Data
Ganeri, Anita, 1961–
Supernatural creatures / by Anita Ganeri and David West.
p. cm. — (Monster fight club)
Includes index.
ISBN 978-1-4488-5197-3 (library binding) — ISBN 978-1-4488-5232-1 (pbk.) —
ISBN 978-1-4488-5233-8 (6-pack)
1. Monsters. 2. Supernatural. I. West, David, 1956- II. Title.
GR825.G36 2012
398'.45—dc22

2011000161
Manufactured in China

CPSIA Compliance Information: Batch #DS1102PK:
For Further Information contact Rosen Publishing, New York,
New York at 1-800-237-9932

CONTENTS

INTRODUCTION

Welcome to the Monster Fight Club! Watch as creatures from myth, legend, and history enter the ring to do battle, often to the death. Have you ever wondered who would win—a werewolf or a vampire? Find out as you enter the weird world of supernatural creatures.

How Does It Work?

There are six monster fights in this book. Before each fight, you will see a profile page for each contestant. This page gives you more information about them. Once you have read the profile pages, you might be able to take a better guess at which monster will win the fight.

WARNING

Blood will be spilled.

The profile pages are crammed with fascinating and bloodcurdling facts about each of the contestants.

Extra illustrations show the contestants in some of their other gory guises so you can build up your own picture.

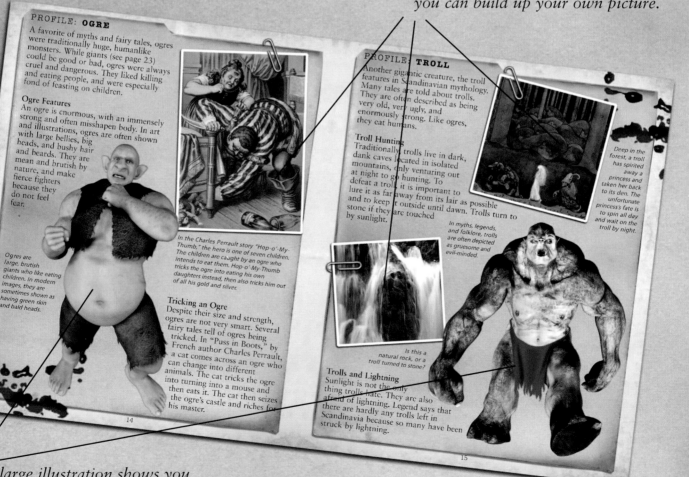

PROFILE: OGRE

A favorite of myths and fairy tales, ogres were traditionally huge, humanlike monsters. While giants (see page 23) could be good or bad, ogres were always cruel and dangerous. They liked killing and eating people, and were especially fond of feasting on children.

Ogre Features

An ogre is enormous, with an immensely strong and often misshapen body. In art and illustrations, ogres are often shown with large bellies, big heads, and bushy hair and beards. They are mean and brutish by nature, and make fierce fighters because they do not feel fear.

Ogres are large, brutish giants who like eating children. In modern images, they are sometimes shown as having green skin and bald heads.

In the Charles Perrault story "Hop-o'-My-Thumb," the hero is one of seven children. The children are caught by an ogre who intends to eat them. Hop-o'-My-Thumb tricks the ogre into eating his own daughters instead, then also tricks him out of all his gold and silver.

Tricking an Ogre

Despite their size and strength, ogres are not very smart. Several fairy tales tell of ogres being tricked. In "Puss in Boots," by French author Charles Perrault, a cat comes across an ogre who can change into different animals. The cat tricks the ogre into turning into a mouse and then eats it. The cat then seizes the ogre's castle and riches for his master.

14

PROFILE: TROLL

Another gigantic creature, the troll features in Scandinavian mythology. Many tales are told about trolls. They are often described as being very old, very ugly, and enormously strong. Like ogres, they eat humans.

Troll Hunting

Traditionally, trolls live in dark, dank caves located in isolated mountains, only venturing out at night to go hunting. To defeat a troll it is important to lure it as far away from its lair as possible and to keep it outside until dawn. Trolls turn to stone if they are touched by sunlight.

Deep in the forest, a troll has spirited away a princess and taken her back to its den. The unfortunate princess's fate is to spin all day and wait on the troll by night.

In myths, legends, and folklore, trolls are often depicted as gruesome and evil-minded.

Is this a natural rock, or a troll turned to stone?

Trolls and Lightning

Sunlight is not the only thing trolls hate. They are also afraid of lightning. Legend says that there are hardly any trolls left in Scandinavia because so many have been struck by lightning.

15

This large illustration shows you each contestant, warts and all, to give you a good idea of their physical features.

Read a chilling account of how each fight progresses in the main text.

Each of the contestants may also fight under a different name, shown here as AKA (Also Known As).

FIGHT 3: OGRE VS. TROLL

Out for an evening's entertainment of child scaring, an ogre stumbles upon a mountain cave—the home of a fearsome troll. The troll has just woken up and is ready to go hunting, but it does not like what it sees. Hiding among the rocks of its lair, it watches the ogre for a while. Then, after the initial shock of seeing such an ugly beast, the troll attacks.

Always ready for a fight, the ogre responds with force. It uproots a tree trunk and begins to bash the troll with it. Roaring in pain, the troll grabs a massive rock and hurls it at the ogre's huge head. This sends the ogre into a dreadful rage, and it lumbers in for the kill.

All night, the two opponents trade blows, with no sign of a winner. The ogre and the troll are well matched—both are immensely strong and immensely mean. Both hate humans, but at this moment, they hate each other more. Just as the ogre begins to tire and looks as if it is losing, dawn breaks. As a shaft of sunlight touches it, the troll turns to stone.

The ogre drags itself to its feet and continues on its way. The fight has given it an appetite. It now has one thing on its mind—to find some humans, hopefully children, to eat.

STATS
OGRE
AKA Ogress (female), Oni (Japan)

STRENGTHS: Very large body and brute strength. Hideously ugly looks can sometimes scares enemies into running away.

WEAKNESSES: A bully who picks on small children, then eats them. Not very intelligent. Can be easily tricked.

STATS
TROLL
AKA Jotunn

STRENGTHS: Superhuman strength and huge size. Good at camouflaging itself so that it can't be spotted.

WEAKNESSES: Slow-witted. Turns to stone if touched by sunlight. Scared of lightning.

WINNER: OGRE

At-a-glance STATS boxes give you vital information about each of the contestants, including their main strengths and weaknesses.

The winner's name is given in this black box in the right-hand corner. Of course, you might not agree.

The Monster Fight

After reading the profile pages for each contestant, turn the page to see the fight. Check out the STATS (Statistics) boxes, which give details of the fighters' main strengths and weaknesses. Then read a blow-by-blow account of the battle, if you dare. The winner, if there is one, is shown in a small black box in the bottom right-hand corner.

PROFILE: **WEREWOLF**

Caught between the worlds of human and animal, a werewolf is a person who can shape-shift into a vicious wolflike beast. Then it prowls the countryside, looking for human prey to kill and eat. Faced with a werewolf's supernatural strength, speed, and cunning, victims have little or no chance of escape.

It is said that only a silver bullet can kill a werewolf.

This German print from the 18th century seems to show a werewolf in the midst of changing from a human to a giant wolf.

Becoming a Werewolf

According to legend, there are several ways of becoming a werewolf. These include being bitten by another werewolf, wearing a wolf skin, drinking water from a wolf's footprint, and sleeping outside during a full moon. A werewolf might also be under a curse.

The transformation from person to wolf takes place under a full moon. As dawn breaks, the werewolf turns back into human form.

Spotting a Werewolf

In wolf form, a werewolf may look and move like a real wolf, or appear more like a half man, half wolf.

Aconitum Lycocto-
num flore Delphini.

Aconitum Lycoctonum
flore luteo.

Wolfsbane can ward off werewolves.

In human form, werewolves can be recognized by their wolflike features, such as hairy faces and hands, and pointed ears. They also have long, clawlike fingernails the color of blood.

PROFILE: **VAMPIRE**

Feared since ancient times, a vampire is a member of the living dead. By day, it rests in a coffin or grave, but at night, as the Sun sets, it leaves its lair in search of victims. Vampires can only survive by drinking human blood. They must return to their graves before dawn breaks–they cannot tolerate sunlight.

Features of Vampires

A typical vampire has a deathly pale face, with bright, clear eyes for hypnotizing its victims. It has long, pointed fangs; very red lips; and long, sharp nails. It casts no shadow and does not have a reflection. Some vampires can shape-shift into animals, most famously bats.

It is thought that garlic, crucifixes and holy water can keep vampires away.

The most famous vampire was Count Dracula. He was based on the infamous Vlad Dracula, who impaled victims on stakes in the 15th century.

Becoming a Vampire

Anyone who is bitten by a vampire is thought to become a vampire after death.

A vampire emerges from its coffin at night.

Vampires bite their victims' necks, then suck out their blood.

FIGHT 1: WEREWOLF VS. VAMPIRE

The venue for tonight's monster fight is an eerie, abandoned cemetery somewhere in eastern Europe. The werewolf prowling among the tombstones is unaware that this is a vampire's resting place. Here the vampire lies in a coffin in a crumbling crypt.

Suddenly, the werewolf hears and smells something moving in the shadows. The vampire has left its lair. With astonishing speed, it leaps at the werewolf. The werewolf gives a bloodcurdling snarl and lashes out with its powerful claws. It hits the vampire in the chest.

Unhurt, the vampire changes into a bat and flies out of the werewolf's reach. The werewolf stumbles to avoid a patch of wolfsbane growing near a tombstone. Taking advantage of its opponent's weakness, the vampire swoops down from behind. Using its wolf-sharp senses, the werewolf picks up the bat's movements, twists around, and strikes. But again the vampire recovers.

Dawn is approaching. As the first rays of sunlight break through, the werewolf starts to weaken and to morph back into human form.

STATS

WEREWOLF
AKA Wolfman, Loup-garou

STRENGTHS: Supernatural power and lightning-fast reflexes, with the cunning and stealth of a wolf. Highly tuned hunting instinct. Excellent senses of hearing and smell.

WEAKNESSES: Cannot tolerate objects made of silver or iron. Hates the sight of wolfsbane and mistletoe. Turns back into human form at daybreak, and before it dies.

The vampire seizes its chance and makes a final attack. It leaps onto the werewolf's back and opens its mouth to reveal its deadly fangs. Suddenly it shrieks in pain. A shaft of sunlight falls across its face. The vampire has not noticed the approaching dawn. It tries to leap into the shadows for safety, but it is too late. It falls to the ground in agony and turns to ashes. Slumped against a gravestone, the werewolf completes its change to human form.

STATS
VAMPIRE
AKA Dracula, Nosferatu

STRENGTHS: Superhuman strength and a killer bite. Can transform into animals so it can travel around quickly and without being seen.

WEAKNESSES: Has to leave its coffin to search for blood, laying itself open to attack. Turns to dust if exposed to sunlight. Shrinks from religious artifacts and garlic. Can be killed by a wooden stake through the heart.

WINNER: WEREWOLF

PROFILE: **ZOMBIE**

The ghoulish stars of horror films, books, and computer games, zombies are the corpses of dead people who have been reanimated (brought back to life). They can move, as if remotely-controlled by someone else, but have no minds of their own.

This bronze relief sculpture shows the Dance of Death, in which a living corpse leads the living in a dance to their graves.

Zombie Images

Zombies can take on different forms. The popular image of a zombie is a human figure with staring eyes and gaping wounds, walking stiffly with arms outstretched. But zombies can also appear as decaying or whole corpses.

Zombies are linked with voodoo, a religion practiced in Haiti. A type of voodoo is also followed in New Orleans. This shop sells voodoo artifacts.

Modern zombies have one aim—to feast on human flesh.

Voodoo Zombies

The idea of zombies comes from the religion of voodoo. It began in West Africa and spread to Haiti, an island in the Caribbean. In voodoo, a zombie is believed to be a corpse that is reanimated by a sorcerer and then becomes the sorcerer's slave.

In voodoo legend, it is said that feeding salt to a zombie will make it return to its grave.

PROFILE: MUMMY

The ancient Egyptians believed in life after death. For a person's soul to survive in the next world, the body had to be preserved. The Egyptians mummified bodies (wrapped them in bandages) to stop them from rotting. Later, makers of horror films gave this idea a twist. Mummies became terrifying creatures that came back to life, looking for revenge.

The ragged, staggering figure of a horror-film mummy

Mummy-Making
In ancient Egypt, a dead body was taken to the embalmers' workshop. There, a cut was made in the side and the organs removed. Then the body was dried out and stuffed with sawdust or linen. Finally, the body was wrapped in bandages and put in a coffin.

The Mummy's Curse
The belief in a mummy's curse comes from writings in some Egyptian tombs. These warned grave robbers to leave the tomb, and its occupant, alone.

In 1922, British archaeologists discovered the tomb of King Tutankhamun, with the king's mummy inside. Afterward, bad luck followed several members of the expedition—was it coincidence or the mummy's curse?

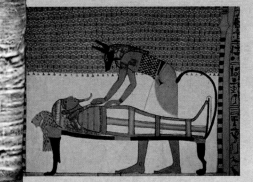

During mummification, the person's organs, such as the heart, lungs, and liver, were removed and placed in special containers, called canopic jars.

The chief embalmer wore a jackal mask to represent the jackal-headed god, Anubis. Anubis was god of the dead.

FIGHT 2: ZOMBIE VS. MUMMY

Escaped from a local museum, where it has lain festering for a hundred years, a mummy staggers into town. It is intent on taking revenge on the robbers who ripped it from its ancient grave. There are no grave robbers in town tonight, but instead the mummy stumbles on one unfortunate inhabitant who has recently been turned into a zombie. Stiff-legged and with unseeing eyes, the zombie has only one goal—to eat human flesh—and it makes a shuffling beeline toward the mummy.

Unfazed, the mummy meets the zombie head-on. It grabs hold of one of the zombie's outstretched arms and tears it off. Even this does not stop the zombie, and it continues its relentless march. But it is no match for the mummy and its superhuman strength. The mummy wrenches off the zombie's other arm, then finally dispatches the zombie by ripping off its head.

The mummy continues its shuffling progress through the town. The night is young, and it has still has to place its deadly curse on those responsible for its fate.

STATS
ZOMBIE
AKA Living Dead

STRENGTHS: Very tough. Can continue to function even if chopped in half. Aggressive and violent. Already dead, so difficult to stop.

WEAKNESSES: Has no mind of its own. Must feed on human flesh. Most effective if part of a crowd. Cannot tolerate salt. Dies once its head is removed.

STATS
MUMMY
AKA (None)

STRENGTHS: Superhuman strength. Comes with a curse that can be deadly. Has no internal organs, so cannot be killed. Some are said to have magical, healing properties.

WEAKNESSES: Slow, sleepwalking gait. Internal organs, such as heart, are kept in canopic jars, which can be destroyed.

WINNER: MUMMY

PROFILE: OGRE

A favorite of myths and fairy tales, ogres were traditionally huge, humanlike monsters. While giants (see page 23) could be good or bad, ogres were always cruel and dangerous. They liked killing and eating people, and were especially fond of feasting on children.

Ogre Features

An ogre is enormous, with an immensely strong and often misshapen body. In art and illustrations, ogres are often shown with large bellies, big heads, and bushy hair and beards. They are mean and brutish by nature, and make fierce fighters because they do not feel fear.

Ogres are large, brutish giants who like eating children. In modern images, they are sometimes shown as having green skin and bald heads.

In the Charles Perrault story "Hop-o'-My-Thumb," the hero is one of seven children. The children are caught by an ogre who intends to eat them. Hop-o'-My-Thumb tricks the ogre into eating his own daughters instead, then also tricks him out of all his gold and silver.

Tricking an Ogre

Despite their size and strength, ogres are not very smart. Several fairy tales tell of ogres being tricked. In "Puss in Boots," by French author Charles Perrault, a cat comes across an ogre who can change into different animals. The cat tricks the ogre into turning into a mouse and then eats it. The cat then seizes the ogre's castle and riches for his master.

PROFILE: **TROLL**

Another gigantic creature, the troll features in Scandinavian mythology. Many tales are told about trolls. They are often described as being very old, very ugly, and enormously strong. Like ogres, they eat humans.

Troll Hunting

Traditionally, trolls live in dark, dank caves located in isolated mountains, only venturing out at night to go hunting. To defeat a troll, it is important to lure it as far away from its lair as possible and to keep it outside until dawn. Trolls turn to stone if they are touched by sunlight.

Deep in the forest, a troll has spirited away a princess and taken her back to its den. The unfortunate princess's fate is to spin all day and wait on the troll by night.

In myths, legends, and folklore, trolls are often depicted as gruesome and evil-minded.

Is this a natural rock, or a troll turned to stone?

Trolls and Lightning

Sunlight is not the only thing trolls hate. They are also afraid of lightning. Legend says that there are hardly any trolls left in Scandinavia because so many have been struck by lightning.

FIGHT 3: OGRE VS. TRULL

Out for an evening's entertainment of child scaring, an ogre stumbles upon a mountain cave—the home of a fearsome troll. The troll has just woken up and is ready to go hunting, but it does not like what it sees. Hiding among the rocks of its lair, it watches the ogre for a while. Then, after the initial shock of seeing such an ugly beast, the troll attacks.

Always ready for a fight, the ogre responds with force. It uproots a tree trunk and begins to bash the troll with it. Roaring in pain, the troll grabs a massive rock and hurls it at the ogre's huge head. This sends the ogre into a dreadful rage, and it lumbers in for the kill.

STATS
OGRE
AKA Ogress (female), Oni (Japan)

STRENGTHS: Very large body and brute strength. Hideously ugly looks can sometimes scare enemies into running away.

WEAKNESSES: A bully who picks on small children, then eats them. Not very intelligent. Can be easily tricked.

All night, the two opponents trade blows, with no sign of a winner. The ogre and the troll are well matched—both are immensely strong and immensely mean. Both hate humans, but at this moment, they hate each other more. Just as the ogre begins to tire and looks as if it is losing, dawn breaks. As a shaft of sunlight touches it, the troll turns to stone.

STATS
TROLL
AKA Jotunn

STRENGTHS: Superhuman strength and huge size. Good at camouflaging itself so that it can't be spotted.

WEAKNESSES: Slow-witted. Turns to stone if touched by sunlight. Scared of lightning.

The ogre drags itself to its feet and continues on its way. The fight has given it an appetite. It now has one thing on its mind—to find some humans, hopefully children, to eat.

WINNER: OGRE

PROFILE: **WIZARD**

Merlinus

An image of Merlin, the great wizard who helped Arthur become king

Myths and legends are filled with references to wizards, or warlocks. A wizard has the gift of magic and uses powerful spells and potions to conjure up the spirits to do his work. Some wizards are born with supernatural powers. Others must learn from their masters.

Wizard Features

Many images of wizards show an elderly man, often with a long beard and flowing hair. Typically, he wears a flowing robe or cloak, decorated with magical signs. Often he carries a staff, which is a symbol of his power. He uses his staff to channel his powers; without it, his magic is greatly weakened.

Some wizards study alchemy, one of the dark arts. They try to turn everyday metals into gold, using the so-called Philosopher's Stone. They also seek to discover the secret of immortality.

Wizard or Sorcerer?

A wizard may practice good or bad magic, but a sorcerer's magic is always malevolent. In their use of the dark arts, sorcerers often work in league with the Devil and are greatly feared. They often wear magical symbols, such as pentacles, around their necks, and carry handbooks of magic, called *grimoires*, which contain spells and recipes for potions.

A wizard casts a spell.

Wizards are skilled at casting all kinds of spells, especially those that change people into animals. Here, a wicked old wizard transforms a princess into a white deer.

A suspected witch being tried in Salem, Massachusetts, in 1692

Silhouetted against the full moon, a witch flies on her broomstick to perform her magic. Like a wizard, she is skilled at casting spells and brewing powerful magic potions in her cauldron. Witches have appeared in myths and folklore from around the world since ancient times. Despite their reputation, they are not always evil, old crones. A "white" witch can sometimes undo the mischief and mayhem caused by a "black" witch.

A witch's traditional form of transportation is a broomstick.

Spotting a Witch

Besides black robes and pointed hats, witches are said to have a mark on their skin called the Devil's mark. It is a sign left by the Devil when a witch makes a pact with him. Witches are also associated with animals, especially cats and bats, known as familiars.

A witch is burned at the stake.

Witches often keep cats as familiars.

Witch Hunts

In the 16th and 17th centuries, people became terrified of witches. Many suspected witches were hunted down and put on trial. If they were found guilty, they were hanged or burned at the stake. The most famous witch trials took place in Salem, Massachusetts (above left).

FIGHT 4: WIZARD VS. WITCH

After centuries of conflict, a witch and a wizard finally meet in a fight to the end. The night is pitch dark, and a looming full moon provides the perfect backdrop to their contest. Dressed in long, flowing robes the color of midnight, and covered in magical symbols, the two take up their positions. Both contestants are well versed in the ancient art of magic, but they know that tonight's encounter will test their powers to the very limit.

The witch chants an

STATS
WITCH
AKA Hag, Banshee, Kitsune-mochi (Japan)

STRENGTHS: Can use powerful magic, using spells and potions. Able to fly on a broomstick.

WEAKNESSES: Easily spotted and hunted down. Powerless against witch finders.

incantation to raise the spirits, and hurls a spell at the wizard, but he is ready and combats it easily. Now it is his turn. Quick as a flash, the witch traces a magic circle around herself to protect herself from whatever the wizard may conjure up. But the wizard raises his staff high into the air, then stamps it three times on the ground. The circle vanishes, and the witch is left dangerously exposed. Summoning up all her powers, she unleashes an even more potent spell. Again, the wizard is ready.

Stats
WIZARD
AKA Warlock, Sorcerer

STRENGTHS: Skilled in magic and can use spells and potions. Can summon up powerful spirits to do his bidding. Able to shape-shift and become invisible.

WEAKNESSES: Witches. Stripped of power if he loses or breaks his staff.

The fight reaches a deadlock. Summoning all of their ancient knowledge, the contestants make one last attempt to snatch victory. This time, they hurl a similar spell at each other, which changes the witch into a cat and the wizard into a rat. The cat has the advantage—its powers are far greater than the rat's. With a spine-tingling yowl, it lunges at the rat and chases it into a stinking sewage drain.

WINNER: WITCH

PROFILE: **DWARF**

Short of stature, but immensely strong, dwarfs feature in many myths, fairy tales, and fantasy tales. They are hard-working and can be wise, but they are also proud and powerful. Some possess magical powers which they use in their work and warfare.

Dwarf Worlds

Legend says that dwarfs usually live deep beneath the ground in caves and tunnels. Many are miners and metalworkers, digging out precious metals and gemstones, and forging them into magical swords and other weapons for the gods and heroes. In Norse mythology, dwarfs make a magic spear for the god Odin, and a magic hammer for the god Thor.

Dwarfs are skilled at metalwork. The dwarf Regin forged Gram, the sword used by the Norse hero Sigurd to slay the dragon Fafnir.

The Norse goddess Freyja visits dwarfs working underground.

Dwarf Features

Traditionally, a dwarf looks like a small, stockily built old man with a bushy beard. He may be shown wearing armor and carrying a weapon, such as a hammer or an ax. In some stories, dwarfs are kind and helpful. More often, though, they can be spiteful and deceitful, or even hostile.

Some of the best-known dwarfs appear in fairy tales such as "Snow White and the Seven Dwarfs." The story is a popular theme for films, books, and plays.

Modern images of dwarfs often show them as warriors dressed in chain mail and carrying hammers or axes.

PROFILE: GIANT

In myths and legends, gigantic, humanlike beings take many roles. Some giants appear as bringers of chaos. They do battle against the great gods and heroes, who in turn try to restore order to the world. Others are seen as forces of nature, forming islands and mountains, and causing disasters such as earthquakes. Some provide opponents for giant slayers, brave warriors trying to make a name for themselves.

Giants attack the gods of Olympia in the battle known as the Gigantomachy.

Giant Features

Along with their enormous size, giants are also extremely strong, capable of uprooting trees and hurling huge rocks over long distances. They take great strides across the countryside, and have loud, booming voices. Giants may be good or evil, and can be dim-witted or smart.

Using his speed against the giant's slowness, King Arthur was able to dodge the blows of the giant's club. He finally killed the giant when it was blinded by blood running into its eyes.

Giants are often shown as nasty brutes who eat humans.

Stories of Giants

Giants are popular characters in myths and fairy tales. In Greek myth, the Gigantes were a race of giants and the sons of Gaia, goddess of the Earth. Gaia fought with Zeus, king of the gods of Olympus, resulting in an epic battle between the giants and gods, called the Gigantomachy. Because the giants could not be killed by the gods, the gods called on the hero, Herakles who was half human. He killed off the giants one by one.

In "The Brave Little Tailor," a German fairy tale from the Brothers Grimm, a tailor outwits two giants by setting them against each other.

FIGHT 5: DWARF VS. GIANT

On a quest to find metal for a magical sword, a dwarf wanders into a giant's territory. Used to living deep underground, the dwarf has become disoriented in the open. The dwarf hopes that his magical armor will hide him but the giant has already sniffed him out. Usually, the giant wouldn't bother with such small fry but he is hungry and the dwarf looks like easy meat. The giant reaches down and grabs, but the dwarf is much too quick for him. Dodging out of the way, the dwarf summons up all his strength and brings his hammer down on the giant's fingers.

STATS
GIANT
AKA Gigante, Jotun, Etin

STRENGTHS: Very big and very strong. Keen sense of smell.

WEAKNESSES: Slow-moving and clumsy. Can be slow-witted and easy to trick.

STATS
DWARF
AKA Uldra (Arctic), Barbegazi (Alps)

STRENGTHS: Has superhuman strength. Likes to fight and is very proud. May wear magical armor. Skilled at using hammers and axes.

WEAKNESSES: Usually lives under-ground. Small stature. Can be stubborn.

Howling in pain, the giant booms out a warning. He is used to fighting the gods and is not about to be outmaneuvered by a dwarf. Again he tries to catch the dwarf, and again, the dwarf escapes his clutches by running through the giant's legs. Despite his size, the dwarf is strong and nimble—the giant has met his match. The dwarf knows that the giant is beaten. He raises his hammer one last time and brings it down hard on the giant's foot. The giant has had enough and hobbles away to lick his wounds.

WINNER: DWARF

25

PROFILE: **SKIN-WALKER**

Of all the supernatural fighters in this book, the skin-walker is one of the most terrifying. A creature from Native American (Navajo) myth, it can shape-shift into any animal it chooses. In disguise, it preys on humans, stealing people's souls by staring into their eyes.

Skin Wearer

A skin-walker can shape-shift into an animal by wearing its skin. Most commonly, it is seen as a coyote, wolf, crow, or fox. In each form it takes on the animal's characteristics, such as a wolf's cunning or a coyote's speed and strength.

In Norse myth, a berserker is a warrior who wears a bearskin. Like a bear, he is immensely strong and a ferocious fighter.

A modern image of a skin walker shows a creature that is half human, half coyote.

This Navajo man in ceremonial dress may be a yeenaaldlooshii, *or skin-walker.*

Magical Powers

Skin-walkers seek out their human prey at night, banging on walls and windows, and breaking into houses. They are also able to mimic human voices to lure their victims out of the safety of their homes. To control their victims, they fire magic charms from blowpipes. These charms may be beads of human bone or sometimes even rattlesnakes. Very little can harm a skin-walker—they are usually too fast to be caught.

A bullet dipped in ash is the only thing that can kill a skin-walker.

PROFILE: RAKSHASA

Demonic creatures appear in stories from around the world. They represent evil in the battle against good. In Hindu and Buddhist mythology, these demons are called rakshasas. They are ferocious-looking monsters that have been reborn as demons because they have been particularly wicked in a previous life. Rakshasas have sharp teeth and venomous fingernails. They like to feast on human flesh and can take possession of humans. They are also illusionists and shape-shifters, making them very dangerous opponents.

In the Ramayana *Ravana is the ten-headed demon king of Lanka (Sri Lanka). He was feared for being a greedy and cruel ruler.*

In Hindu Myths

Rakshasas appear in many Hindu myths and texts. They are feared warriors and often make their appearance when a battle is at its worst, sometimes using secret weapons against their enemies. In the epic poem the *Ramayana*, Sita, wife of the god, Rama, is kidnapped by Ravana.

A rakshasa warrior fights with a sword in a temple painting.

A modern image of a rakshasa

A painting of The Battle of Lanka, in which Rama's army of monkeys beat Ravana's army of rakshasas to win back Rama's wife, Sita.

FIGHT 6: SKIN-WALKER VS. RAKSHASA

In a strange warp in the fabric of time and space, the worlds of two supernatural creatures collide. In a particularly gruesome battle, a rakshasa comes face to face with a Navajo skin-walker. A vicious fighter, the rakshasa charges the skin-walker, hoping to slice it to pieces with his venomous nails. But the skin-walker has taken on the characteristics of a coyote and is too fast and agile for the rakshasa to catch.

The rakshasa is a feared warrior, used to fighting epic battles against the gods. But it has never faced a foe as cunning as the skin-walker. In an effort to win the advantage, the rakshasa uses its magical powers to possess the skin-walker's body. For a while, this tactic looks as if it is working, as the skin-walker writhes in agony. But even this is not enough—the skin-walker regains control and possesses the rakshasa back.

STATS
SKIN-WALKER
AKA Yeenaaldlooshii

STRENGTHS: Fast and almost impossible to catch. Can shape shift into any animal form. Can possess human beings by staring into their eyes.

WEAKNESSES: Can be killed by bullets dipped in white ash.

Now that the skin-walker has the upper hand, it goes in for the kill. Eyes glowing, it circles the rakshasa, then lashes out with its razor-sharp claws. It delivers a terrible blow to the rakshasa, which stumbles but soon gets back on its feet. Using its superhuman strength, the rakshasa launches one final attack.

STATS
RAKSHASA
AKA Demon, Ghoul

STRENGTHS: Venomous fingernails and sharp teeth. Fierce and powerful warriors. Able to possess human beings. They are also shape–shifters and illusionists.

WEAKNESSES: No match against the gods and the forces of good.

The only way to kill the skin-walker is with a bullet dipped in ash and it shows no sign of weakening. Instead, it pulls out a blowpipe and fires a volley of bone beads, which burrow into the rakshasa's skin and kills it.

WINNER: SKIN-WALKER

CREATE YOUR OWN FIGHT

You might not agree with some of the fight results in this book. If that's the case, try writing your own fight report based on the facts supplied on the profile pages? Better still, choose your own monsters and create your own supernatural creature fight.

Monster Research
Once you have chosen your two creatures, do some research about them using books and the Internet. You can make them fairly similar, such as the ogre and the troll, or very different, such as the dwarf and the giant.

Stats Boxes
Think about stats for each monster. Find out about any other names for the AKA section. Make a list of strengths—such as size, the ability to shape-shift or secret weapons—and also a list of weaknesses, such as how it can be killed.

In the Ring
Pick a setting where your monsters are likely to meet, and write a blow-by-blow account of how you imagine the fight might happen. Think of each monster's key characteristics, along with their strengths and weaknesses. Remember, there doesn't always have to be a winner.

Supernatural Creatures
This list includes some other supernatural creatures that might want to join the Monster Fight Club:
Angel
Banshee
Bogeyman
Boggart
Demon
Djinn
Elf
Gargoyle
Ghost
Ghoul
Goblin
Hombre Caiman
Leprechaun
Mare
Mothman
Tengu
Wendigo

An angel doing battle with a demon might be a good fight for you to start with.

GLOSSARY

alchemy (AL-kuh-mee)
A magical process used to try to turn ordinary metals into gold and to make an elixir of immortality.

archaeologist (ahr-kee-AH-luh-jist)
A person who studies the past by looking at ancient artifacts and the ruins of buildings.

dwarf (DWORF)
A short, humanlike creature that is immensely strong and usually lives underground.

embalmer (im-BAHL-mur)
A person who treats a dead body with oils and other preservatives to prevent it rotting.

illusionists (ih-LOOZH-nists)
People or beings who have the power to make things appear to be what they are not.

immortality (ih-mor-TAH-lih-tee)
Never dying but living for ever.

malevolent (muh-LEH-vuh-lent)
Malicious; wishing evil on others.

mummy (MUH-mee)
A body that has been wrapped in bandages or dried out to prevent it rotting away.

ogre (OH-gur)
A huge humanlike creature that is cruel and enormously strong.

rakshasa (RAHK-shahs)
A demonic creature from Hindu and Buddhist mythology. Usually evil and ferocious looking.

shape-shift (SHAYP-shift)
Magically change shape from a human into an animal, or from an animal to an animal.

skin-walker (SKIN-wah-kur)
A creature from Native American myth that can shape-shift into many different animals.

supernatural (soo-per-NA-chuh-rul)
Magical beings that cannot be explained by physical or scientific laws.

troll (TROHL)
A gigantic, mythological creature, often old and ugly, from Scandinavia.

vampire (VAN-pyr)
A member of the living dead that drinks blood and can shape-shift into a bat.

werewolf (WIR-wulf)
A person who can change shape and become a wolflike beast.

witch (WICH)
A woman skilled in magic and casting spells and is associated with cats, cauldrons and broomsticks.

wizard (WIH-zerd)
A man skilled in magic who uses spells and potions to conjure up the spirits.

zombie (ZOM-bee)
Corpses that have been brought back to life and operate under someone else's command.

INDEX

Web Sites
Due to the changing nature of Internet links, PowerKids Press has developed an online list of Web sites related to the subject of this book. This site is updated regularly. Please use this link to access the list:
www.powerkidslinks.com/mfc/super/